COLLAPSING THE DIVIDE
GENDER EQUALITY AND EQUITY

Adam J. Johnson

Contents

CHAPTER 1: INTRODUCTION

Gender—our inner sense of being male, female, a combination, or neither—is fundamental to one's identity and expression. Gender shapes our interactions, relationships, opportunities, and challenges throughout life. While gender may feel innate, many aspects of gender identity and expression are socially constructed over time. Rigid gender norms and inequality emerged through particular historical and cultural forces.

This book provides an in-depth look at the evolution of gender issues, persisting pain points, and the vision for a more equal future. First, we must ground this discussion in key terminology and concepts.

Sex vs. Gender Biological classifications of male and female reflect one's sex, based on reproductive anatomy and chromosomes. Gender encompasses the complex social, cultural, and psychological traits linked to masculinity and femininity. While sex is biologically determined, gender identity and presentation are largely socially conditioned. Mismatch often exists between one's inner gender and biological sex.

Gender Identity, Roles, and Expression Gender identity refers to one's inner sense of self as male, female, a blend, or neither. Gender roles comprise the behaviors, attitudes, and personality traits expected from each sex within a society. Gender expression relates to how one outwardly presents their gender through clothing, hairstyles, voice, mannerisms, and interests. Individuals should have the freedom to explore and express their gender identity in ways that feel right for them.

Brief History of Gender Issues

While each culture defines gender norms differently, most human civilizations have tended toward binary male-female gender systems and hierarchies. Here is a brief overview of how fundamental understandings of gender have evolved over time:

Ancient Cultures - While today's society predominately operates within a male-female gender binary, many ancient cultures had more fluid conceptions of gender that accepted and even venerated those living outside binary norms. In ancient Sumerian civilization, priests known as gala worshipped the goddess Inanna, dressing and living as women despite male anatomy. Likewise, in ancient Assyria, the goddess Ishtar was worshipped by third-gender, or non-binary, priests called assinnu who occupied a revered spiritual role. In some North American indigenous cultures, people known as Two-Spirits fluidly crossed male and female societal roles. Ancient Egyptian mythology contains accounts of their gods switching between male and female forms, including the deity Atum transforming into the goddess Iusaaset in order to facilitate creation. The ancient Greeks, Romans, and Chinese cultures also reference transgender and gender fluid figures in their mythologies and legends. While details differ between regions, many early civilizations acknowledged a spectrum of gender identities tied to local religious customs and social structures. Gender variance was not unheard of, but simply accepted as another thread in the human experience. Only later did more rigid binary conceptions of gender develop and become culturally dominant under various religious and political forces, marginalizing those falling outside the male-female norms. Examining history reveals the diverse understandings of gender possible in societies.

Middle Ages - The Middle Ages saw a hardening of attitudes toward gender roles and expression as the Christian church gained dominance in Europe. While some early saints were reputed to have passed as men, increased emphasis was put on maintaining the gender binary. Women were excluded from religious leadership roles and political power. Expectations of chastity and purity were placed heavily on women along with dress codes enforcing modesty. Men's and women's spheres grew increasingly separate, with women relegated to the domestic realm. Those displaying gender ambiguity through roles or clothing were marginalized as unnatural or heretical. While fluidity had been tolerated in pagan societies, the Church strictly policed any perceived transgressions of binary gender boundaries. Accusations of sodomy were used to persecute certain male behaviors. As Church authority permeated society, norms hardened around masculine strength, reason and power contrasted with feminine emotion, nurturing and deference to male authority. This Christian moral ethos formed the foundation of modern Western gender ideology. While variation always exists, the Middle Ages largely stamped out societies' earlier openness toward fluidity in gender expression and social roles.

Industrial Revolution - Factory jobs redefined gender roles. "Cult of Domesticity" confined middle/upper class women to the home.

Early 1900s - The early 20th century marked growing restlessness with Victorian era gender constraints. Roles for women began to expand, sparked by involvement in social reform causes like temperance and urban missions. Women increasingly worked outside the home out of either necessity or choice. The suffrage movement also brought expansions in women's political participation. While conservative norms around feminine domesticity persisted, pioneering shifts allowing women into higher education, careers like medicine and law, and the public sphere of activism took hold. Some women adopted practical, comfortable clothing like bloomers that enabled broader life participation. Meanwhile, the scientific study of gender and sexuality advanced, with early researchers like Magnus Hirschfeld pioneering work on diverse sexual orientations and transgender identity. While social stigma persisted, urban gay and lesbian subcultures quietly grew. The seeds of Women's Liberation, Gay Liberation and other gender identity movements of the 1960s-70s were planted during the early 20th century shifts toward modern womanhood. While slow and geographically uneven, early progress was made in how gender was conceived, enacted and studied during this transitional period.

1960s - The 1960s marked a pivotal time when ideas of fixed, innate gender differences came under scrutiny. The emergence of second-wave feminism challenged assumptions around women's roles and capabilities. Betty Friedan's 1963 book The Feminine Mystique exposed the discontent of domestic suburban womanhood. Female empowerment was embraced by the civil rights, anti-war and black power movements of the era as well. Academically, psychologists like Sandra Bem developed theories of gender as socially constructed rather than biologically determined. Anthropologists such as Margaret Mead highlighted how gender norms varied cross-culturally. Women increasingly pursued nontraditional careers and lifestyles thanks to growing college access and the birth control pill. While the 1950s marked extreme gender conservatism in America, seeds of change were planted in the 60s through dissenting political activism, literature and science. Core concepts of modern gender theory, queer studies and the fight against binary gender constraints took root. This created an ideological foundation for the evolution of gender politics and identity conceptualization in the later decades of the 20th century.

1990s - Rise of academic gender/queer studies programs. Broader understanding of gender as nonbinary.

2000s - The early 2000s ushered in growing mainstream visibility and acceptance of transgender identities. While transgender rights activism had begun decades prior, a cultural tipping point occurred as media representation increased. Films like Boys Don't Cry and Transamerica and TV shows like The L Word portrayed sympathetic transgender protagonists. High profile transgender figures also came to prominence, like politician Georgina Beyer and musician Wendy Carlos. The Internet provided information and community for questioning youth, facilitating transitions. Medical knowledge advanced as well, improving access to gender-affirming treatments. Changing social attitudes led to policy shifts like more robust non-discrimination protections and hate crime laws covering gender identity. Companies also proactively created trans-inclusive health benefits and diversity policies. While acceptance remains gradual and geographically uneven, the early 2000s marked a turning point as binary conceptions of gender were more widely questioned. Younger generations in particular demonstrate greater comfort with fluidity. The groundwork was laid for present-day notions of gender as a multidimensional spectrum rather than a rigid male/female binary. Work remains, but culture moved toward transgender liberation.

While imbalances have improved in recent decades, full gender liberation requires undoing millennia of restrictive conditioning. The remaining chapters will dive deeper into where key gender inequality issues persist today and how we can envision more inclusive, identity-affirming institutions for tomorrow.

Why Gender Equality Matters

At a basic level, gender determines social status and access to rights and resources. Rigid gender hierarchies directly fuel inequality and oppression. Dismantling unjust gender constraints benefits everyone—male, female, and nonbinary folks alike. More broadly speaking, gender equality:

- Creates a fairer, more ethical society where all people can equally develop their capabilities and express themselves.
- Doubles the pool of human talent we draw from to solve problems and make discoveries.
- Enables men to develop their whole selves, not just strengths associated with narrow male stereotypes.
- Uplifts family structures by sharing domestic responsibilities.
- Boosts economies as more women join the workforce.
- Helps people form deeper human connections unencumbered by artificial constraints.
- Allows all identities to be honored for their differences and contributions.
- Opens up future possibilities by removing limits on how people should live based on gender.

In the past, pursuing gender equality was viewed as a "women's issue." However, releasing people from the grip of gender oppression ultimately uplifts everyone. This work involves understanding the lingering effects of historical inequality, centering marginalized voices, and envisioning a society where all genders can exercise their rights, follow their talents, and live authentically.

While no nation has yet eliminated gender-based constraints, progress occurs incrementally through changing attitudes and norms. From workplace policies to healthcare access, this book will highlight key areas for continuing that work globally. With compassion and perseverance, we can move beyond the gender-based pain points of the past toward a future of equity and freedom. The task now is to listen, learn, and work together to turn that vision into reality through systemic change.

Adam J. Johnson

Chapter 2: The Persistence of Gender Stereotypes and Roles

While gender norms have loosened over time, rigid expectations and stereotypes still persist around masculinity and femininity. From an early age, children absorb overt and covert messages about gender-linked traits and behaviors. Though not universally true, these socially-shaped beliefs continue to influence perceptions, opportunities, and relationships.

Examining the impacts of limiting gender assumptions is crucial to creating a more expansive and equitable society. This chapter will dive into examples of residual gender stereotypes and consider steps we can take to broaden notions of manhood and womanhood.

<u>Examples of Restrictive Gender Stereotypes</u>

Gender stereotypes comprise the character traits and behaviors expected from men and women due to their sex. Here are some stubborn stereotypes that still shape attitudes today:

For Men:

One major restrictive stereotype men face is that they must be stoic and suppress emotion. From a young age, boys face messaging that anger and aggression are acceptable but that displays of sadness, vulnerability, or tenderness go against norms of masculinity. Men deal with the same range of human emotions as women, but are pressured to bottle up feelings, only displaying strength. This not only causes psychological distress but limits male emotional intelligence and the ability to form deep relationships. Rigid norms dictate men should stand completely independently rather than seek or accept help.

Relatedly, men are expected to embrace domination, aggression, and brute strength as part of manhood. They must exude confidence at all times and never show weakness. Backing down from confrontation and being gentle or collaborative get perceived as feminine. Manhood becomes defined in relation to wielding power over others, fostering bullying and control. Violence becomes more likely as disputes get settled through aggression rather than peaceful, mature conflict resolution.

Despite more men nurturing their children today, societal norms still position caregiving as a predominantly feminine trait. Mothers are expected to be the warm, gentle, loving caregivers while fathers play a secondary role focused on physical play or discipline. Nurturance and affection get portrayed as more natural for women. Men hesitant to hug, kiss, wipe a nose or sing lullabies to children out of fear of seeming unmanly. Vulnerability, empathy, and close emotional connections become deemed off-limits.

Rigid norms also persist around male activities, style of dress, and self-expression based on outdated views of masculinity. Men face ridicule for pursuits like art, poetry, dance, or care-oriented careers stereotyped as feminine. Gender lines even permeate colors, with blue strictly coded for boys and pink for girls. Criticism awaits men who dare defy conventions by acting flamboyant, wearing bright colors or adopting non-heteronormative style. While gradually changing, narrow conceptions of manhood limit identity expression.

Outdated assumptions also posit men as highly sexed beings focused on sexual conquest. Masculinity becomes precariously tied to sexual virility and prowess. Men feel shamed for disinterest in sex or inability to "perform." At the same time, norms of female purity persist, furthering outdated Madonna-whore dichotomies. Men face pressure to conform to playboy behavior, objectify women's bodies, and treat sex as transactional to prove manhood.

Finally, men are still expected to be the financial providers protecting and materially supporting their wives and families. Even as more women work and gender roles evolve, remnants of the male breadwinner model remain. Men hesitant to have a wife who earns more out of fear of losing dominance. Admitting vulnerability around providing fails to align with masculine norms. Outdated conceptions of men as solely responsible for a family's financial stability linger.

For Women:

One major female stereotype is that women are inherently more emotional, sensitive, and anxious than men. Displays of sadness, nervousness, sentimentality or hysteria get explained away as simply part of female biology and psychology rather than rational responses to experiences. By contrast, the same emotions in men appear alarming as violations of male stoicism. Women get labeled as irrational, moody, and controlled by their emotions. This emotional profiling results in dismissal of women's concerns, abilities, and objections as overly sensitive. Emotional displays by men may be censured, but brave vulnerability in women gets cast as weakness and instability.

Relatedly, norms of femininity pressure women to be polite, gentle, and deferential. Expressing anger, frustration, or boldness crosses boundaries of expected female submission. Women face reproach for speaking bluntly, voicing confident opinions, asserting rights, or achieving visible success outdistancing men. Doing so runs counter to gender conditioning toward quietly supporting others. Women taught to shrink themselves, avoid conflict, and not intimidate male egos. Demanding equality or respect breaks unwritten feminine codes constraining assertiveness.

Women also bear disproportionate expectations around nurturing, with motherhood seen as an innate female calling. Maternal instincts and aptitudes for domestic duties get assumed as natural female traits. By contrast, competence in intellectual professional domains traditionally filled by men is not presumed. Women encouraged to curtail ambitions to prioritize having children and caring for home/family. Doing otherwise defies powerful norms of womanhood.

Strict beauty norms and perpetual youthfulness also permeate standards for feminine worth. Flaws must be eliminated or hidden. Women judged daily on appearance in ways unfamiliar to men. Eating disorders, anxiety, and depression often stem from the objectification of female bodies to exacting, airbrushed standards. Women are not granted the same dignity to age and have value unrelated to appearance.

Powerful norms also persist around suitable "feminine" interests, activities, and self-expression. Women who demonstrate stereotypical male traits like ambition, dominance, assertiveness, high libido or physical prowess face criticism for violating gender mandates. Women in leadership deemed pushy or bitchy. Athleticism masculinizes women. While norms are relaxing, women still pressured to conform to restrictive ideals stifling authentic identity.

Lastly, inaccurate assumptions of female intellectual inferiority compared to men continue today. This surfaces in women's underrepresentation in STEM fields, higher education faculty, and positions of authority. Lingering bias subtly questions women's competence, rationality, and capacity to lead. Pockets of paternalism toward the "fairer sex" endure alongside more overt discrimination. True equality requires dismantling embedded notions of women as the lesser sex.

Consequences of Binary Gender Roles

In reality, gender exists on a fluid spectrum. Nonetheless, social institutions pressure individuals to conform to binary masculine and feminine ideals. Some key consequences include:

Reduces identity expression - Rigid norm enforcement pressures people to hide or change their authentic selves to fit in.

Impacts relationships - Adhering to stereotypes distorts communications and intimacy between romantic partners.

Influences career paths - Gender socialization pushes men and women into particular educational subjects and jobs.

Hinders work opportunities - Those who defy stereotypes can experience bias in hiring, promotion, compensation, etc.

Leads to gender-based harassment - Aggression often stems from hostile policing of male and female roles.

Increases discrimination - Transphobia, homophobia, and sexism all link to enforcing strict conceptions of gender.

Harms mental health - Challenging norms elicits stress. Suppressing identity is linked with anxiety and depression.

Entrenches inequality - Confining gender roles historically served to maintain women's inferior social position.

Though individuals vary greatly within each sex,

either/or categorization remains commonplace. However, the lines separating manhood and womanhood grow fainter over time. Younger generations increasingly embrace more fluidity, demonstrating that change is possible.

Steps to Loosen Gender Role Rigidity

Dismantling the harmful impacts of gender stereotypes requires work on many fronts, including:

Fundamentally, dismantling the harmful impacts of gender stereotypes and roles must start from an early age. Schools and families should teach children to think critically about the gender-based messages they receive and avoid reflexively socializing expectations linked to one gender. Literature, media, activities, and culture must show the full range of masculinities and femininities. Children can then grow valuing diversity and humanity over limitations of gender. Actively humanizing people across the full gender spectrum plants the seeds for a future generation embracing fluidity.

Awareness and introspection are also key at an individual level. We must train our eyes to recognize subtle forms of gender policing that persist in day-to-day conversations, workplace dynamics, media narratives, and our own cognitive patterns. Catching our instinctive social biases and projections is the first step toward change. Only through continual self-checking of assumptions can we prevent regressing into restrictive norms. We must also push each other for growth through calling out language or actions reinforcing outdated gender constraints with empathy.

From schools to social media, we need more narratives and role models celebrating positive examples of gender role defiance. The more girls and boys see others excelling in spaces culturally marked for the opposite gender, the more they come to see possibilities beyond limits. We must loudly praise multidimensionality and those embracing their full humanity regardless of societal gendering. Countering singular images of masculinity and femininity with poetic stories of every kind of life path chips away at stereotypes.

Institutions from workplaces to government must also live up to the task. Local, state and federal laws and workplace regulations supporting equal pay, flexible gender roles, inclusive language, gender neutral facilities, and protections from identity discrimination model the change needed. Companies can set an example through implementing trans-inclusive diversity, bathroom access, benefits, dress code and culture policies. Schools and public services must also demonstrate a commitment to ending gender constraints through both laws and culture.

Given the very forces propping up masculine power and privilege, it is crucial that men themselves embrace feminism and gender equality as empowering rather than threatening. Organizations like the Mankind Project work to help men move beyond limits of the masculine stereotypes trapping them from inner growth. Male voices on gender can hold unique power given cultural imbalances in authority. We need more men to step up as vocal allies.

None of these steps alone can dismantle generations of rigid gender socialization, but combined they hold promise. Critically, the work must occur simultaneously within societal systems, cultural narratives, workplace policies, legislation, and our individual beliefs. With teamwork and moral conviction, more equitable and liberating conceptions of gender are possible.

With compassion and courage, we can open our minds to the diversity of masculinities and femininities that enrich our world. Our shared humanity transcends limited gender stereotypes. Though work remains, progress toward true gender liberation is underway one mind at a time.

CHAPTER 3: TRANSGENDER AND NON-BINARY IDENTITIES

Beyond the male-female binary, gender diverse identities exist across a broad and fluid spectrum. People whose gender identity differs from their assigned sex at birth face unique challenges in a cisnormative society.

This chapter provides an overview of key terms, barriers, and the ongoing fight for transgender rights and inclusion. Sharing lived experiences dispels myths, builds empathy, and motivates further progress.

The Gender Identity Spectrum

Gender identity encompasses one's inner sense of being male, female, a mix, or neither. While assigned sex and identity often align, transgender (trans) and non-binary identities demonstrate a spectrum exists.

Key identity terms include:

Gender identity encompasses one's inner sense of being male, female, a mix, or neither. <u>Cisgender</u> refers to when one's gender identity aligns with their sex assigned at birth based on anatomical characteristics. Most people are cisgender, and thus experience relative ease navigating a culture that assumes their gender aligns with binary societal expectations.

<u>Transgender</u>, or trans, is an umbrella term for people whose inner gender identity or expression differs from societal norms tied to their assigned sex. Many transgender individuals identify fully as male or female, but transition socially or medically to align physical characteristics and public presentation with their identity. However, some trans individuals embrace a more non-binary gender.

<u>Non-binary</u> refers to gender identities that fall outside the conventional binaries of male or female. There is incredible diversity within the non-binary community. Some common terms include genderfluid, for those whose gender shifts between identities over time or in different contexts. Agender refers to having no specific gender identity. Bigender folks identify with two genders simultaneously. The possibilities are endless across the gender spectrum.

When an individual's gender assigned at birth clashes with their identity, this can cause significant psychological distress known as gender dysphoria. Attempts to suppress inner identity creates profound discontent. While not all transgender individuals experience dysphoria to disabling levels, it remains a real concern needing compassionate care.

Gender affirming refers to the social or medical transition process to bring one's outward presentation and physical body into alignment with inner gender identity. This can include changing name, pronouns, style of dress, taking hormones, or pursuing various surgeries. The steps taken are unique to each person.

Two offensive practices that should be avoided are deadnaming and misgendering. Deadnaming refers to calling a transgender person by the name they used prior to transitioning, which negates their identity. Misgendering means referring to someone using pronouns or language incongruent with their gender identity. Doing so communicates invalidation of who they are. Respecting transgender individuals involves honoring their names and pronouns.

Understanding this terminology provides a helpful window into the nuanced gender journeys of many people we encounter each day. Fundamentally, we must affirm however individuals describe or express themselves. There is courage in living one's truth in a society with rigid binary conceptions. Expanding our language and perspectives makes space for that courage.

These broad terms demonstrate the diversity of possible gender journeys. Identity can be complex and fluid. What matters most is affirming how individuals describe themselves.

Barriers and Discrimination

Trans and non-binary people face marginalization across settings:

Bathrooms/facilities – Forced use based on assigned sex denies dignity and safety. Gender neutral options are slowly increasing.

Sports – Restrictive leagues, claims of unfair "advantages," ignorance of science on performance.

Documentation – Difficulty changing gender markers on IDs causes "outing" and problems accessing services.

Healthcare – Finding trans-affirming providers is challenging. Gender affirming treatments may not be covered.

Workplace – Bias in hiring/promotion, lack of inclusive policies, or harassment around gender expression.

Housing/shelters – Gender segregation marginalizes trans and non-binary individuals when seeking refuge.

Violence – High murder rates particularly impact trans

women of color. "Trans panic defense" still raised in court.

Public spaces – Routine harassment, mocking, and policing of gender expression. Fear of physical attack.

Military – Despite some loosening of restrictions, trans individuals still face service barriers.

Media representation – When present at all, trans people portrayed negatively or used as punchlines.

Such systemic barriers result in disproportionate rates of unemployment, poverty, homelessness, and suicide within the transgender community. Cisgender privilege enables avoiding daily challenges around identity and thriving in a society catered to binary norms.

Pushing for Rights and Inclusion

Despite obstacles, the transgender rights movement continues making strides through activism:

Despite facing countless obstacles, the transgender rights movement continues making gradual but meaningful progress through advocacy and activism. At the forefront stand networks of transgender-led organizations like the National Center for Transgender Equality, Transgender Law Center, and Transgender Education Network of Texas. Through public education, policy reform initiatives, legal support, and community empowerment programs, the work advances steadily.

Major legislative gains have included passing local, state and federal anti-discrimination protections covering employment, housing, healthcare, banking, and public accommodations. Comprehensive non-discrimination acts remain crucial to prevent identity-based mistreatment. Rights groups have also worked to prohibit "conversion therapy" attempts on minors and enable simplified processes for transgender folks to change gender identity markers on identification documents—removing daily hurdles. Advocacy around equal access to gender-segregated facilities like bathrooms and locker rooms continues as a priority issue as well, though much opposition persists.

From Hollywood to Silicon Valley, media and business worlds are stepping up to increase fair transgender representation. Films like Boys Don't Cry, television series like Pose and Orange is the New Black, and popular YouTube vlogs have humanized authentic trans experiences for mass audiences. High profile transgender figures like athlete Caitlyn Jenner, model Laverne Cox, and author Janet Mock show possibilities to youth. Leading companies now include gender identity in diversity policies and provide transgender-inclusive health benefits.

Public education also continues through awareness campaigns on gender diversity and transgender lives, aiming to build empathy. Supportive corporations, universities, and nonprofits provide compassionate listening spaces and training addressing unconscious bias against trans individuals. While change is gradual, these efforts progressively chip away at stigma.

Healthcare access remains a key domain for improvement. Though insurance coverage has expanded, not all plans cover gender-affirming medical treatments uniformly. Ethical debates persist around youth access to puberty blockers and hormones. However, research shows transgender-competent, affordable healthcare improves mental health outcomes. So, advocates continue working to expand safe, inclusive clinical policies and practices.

At the community level, a growing number of organizations led by transgender individuals provide critical social services and support. Groups like the LA LGBT Center and the Transgender Resource Center of New Mexico operate shelters, offer counseling services, distribute necessities, provide workforce programs, and facilitate community building—lifelines for marginalized populations. While trans individuals continue facing discrimination, resilient networks affirm and uplift lives nationwide.

Powerful Transgender Perspectives and Voices

Trans folks and allies agree that sharing stories is among the best ways to dispel harmful stereotypes and myths. Here are just a few inspiring examples of transgender individuals who boldly speak their truths:

Author Janet Mock – Advocate for trans women with bestselling memoir Redefining Realness and host of the TV show Pose.

Model and actress Laverne Cox – Emmy-nominated role in Orange Is the New Black increased trans representation.

Writer Raquel Willis – Leading voice exploring intersections of race and trans identity. Founder of initiative #BlackTransCircles.

Performer/songwriter Mila Jam – Uses music and videos to increase trans visibility. Started the GenderCool Project spotlighting youth voices.

YouTuber Natalie Wynn – Entertainingly counters misconceptions on her ContraPoints channel. Named one of Time's 25 Most Influential People on the Internet.

Actress Nicole Maines – As transgender teenager on Supergirl became first trans superhero on TV. Wrote memoir Becoming Nicole.

Author Jacob Tobia – Chronicles a non-binary life in memoir Sissy: A Coming-of-Gender Story.

We all have a role to play in transforming society into one of empathy, freedom and safety for people of every gender. While injustice persists, brave transgender voices today inspire hope for positive change. They remind us of our shared humanity transcends limiting binary categories. By elevating these perspectives, we move closer to a culture of true gender inclusion.

Collapsing the Divide

CHAPTER 4: THE GENDER PAY GAP

Despite progress toward workplace equality, data reveals women continue to earn less than men across industries worldwide. The gender pay gap manifests through lower wages for comparable work, reduced career advancement opportunities, and a disproportionate number of women in low-paying fields.

Understanding the complex web of cultural and structural factors fueling the pay gap empowers society to implement solutions. This chapter will examine troubling stats, impacts, and strategies for finally achieving pay equity.

The Persistent Global Pay Gap

According to the Organization for Economic Cooperation and Development (OECD), the average gender wage gap among 42 nations is 13 percent as of 2022. While smaller than the nearly 40 percent gap in 1970, true parity remains elusive.

Here are gender pay gap stats among some major countries:

- United States – 18 percent
- United Kingdom – 15 percent
- Canada – 13 percent
- Australia – 14 percent
- Japan – 23 percent
- France – 12 percent
- Mexico – 17 percent
- India – 22 percent

Within each country, significant occupational variations exist. Women generally face the largest gaps in financial services, engineering, senior management roles, medicine, and technology. Stark gaps also persist across racial/ethnic groups, with minority women suffering double disadvantage.

While explicit wage discrimination is increasingly illegal, most gaps stem from systemic factors we must counteract.

Key Drivers of the Gender Pay Gap

The gender pay gap stems from a complex web of structural and cultural dynamics that intersect to systemically disadvantage women economically compared to men. While some nations have made more progress than others, a stubborn gap between average male and female earnings persists globally. Closing it requires confronting the root causes.

Firstly, cultural nudges from a young age funnel women toward educational subjects and careers that tend to be lower-paid such as teaching, nursing, domestic work, administration, and care-centered fields. Meanwhile, higher-earning domains like technology, finance, sciences, engineering, and leadership remain male-dominated. These trends of occupational gender segregation get shaped early in childhood socialization. Greater gender balance across all fields would equalize pay scales.

Secondly, the lack of supportive workplace policies around parental leave, childcare, and flexible work arrangements disproportionately leads women to reduce hours or drop out of the workforce after having children. The motherhood penalty persists, while fatherhood generally boosts earnings. Companies lacking family-friendly policies inadvertently perpetuate the gap through losing female talent.

Furthermore, household and childcare labor continues falling much more heavily on women regardless of their working status. The daily demands of domestic duties leave women with less time for paid work. Men do not face the same constraints, enabling more continuous career advancement. Sharing these unpaid responsibilities equitably would create more parity.

Additionally, women marginalized on multiple dimensions like race, disability status, sexual orientation, or immigration background face compounding biases impacting their hiring, wages, promotions, and overall advancement. Minority stressors intersect in ways that cannot be disentangled from gender alone.

From early ages, boys and girls absorb different implicit messages around earning power, entitlement, and developing salary negotiation skills. This gendered socialization ripples across the lifespan in work habits. Cultural expectations of female modesty and passivity put them at a bargaining disadvantage.

Conscious and unconscious hiring biases also impede women's career progression and pay. With few objective performance metrics, subjective perceptions of competence, commitment, and promotion potential disadvantage women. Deeply embedded stereotypes portray leadership ability as inherently masculine.

Lastly, pay secrecy allows gender discrimination to remain unchecked and continue unchecked from one job to the next. Salaries generally get viewed as private, but this opacity maintains unequal practices. Greater pay transparency and auditing enables proactive rectification of company disparities.

No single lever completely explains the tenacious gender pay gap. Rather, it emerges through the accumulation of cultural nudges and structural barriers that limit women's earnings across industries worldwide. Holistic solutions must address this full range of forces.

Impacts on Women's Career Prospects

The gender pay gap inflicts financial and psychological harm with ripple effects over the life course:

Reduced savings and wealth – Less disposable income impacts women's ability to save for retirement, purchase property, and build assets. The wealth gap persists into old age.

Career stagnation – Lower pay signals reduced competence or commitment, harming promotion chances. Some scale back ambitions.

Stereotype threat – Pay gaps reinforce notions of

inferior work quality/ability, further shaking confidence and aspirations.

Work-family strain – Women more acutely feel the pressure to choose between career and family as flexible, affordable childcare remains limited.

By curtailing women's socioeconomic power, pay gaps perpetuate historical gendered power differentials both at home and work.

<u>Evidence-Based Strategies to Close the Gap</u>

Research reveals that nations making the most progress toward pay equity implement a multipronged approach engaging governments, employers, and individuals to chip away at the gap from all angles.

Several leading countries now mandate pay gap transparency, requiring organizations above a certain size to publish audited data on gender pay differences. This reporting motivates companies to proactively evaluate and address compensation gaps before forced to make problems public. It also informs worker negotiations. The governments of Australia, the United Kingdom, and many European Union members have been at the forefront of this policy shift.

In a similar vein, some nations are beginning to require or strongly incentivize equal salary audits by third party experts. Rather than waiting passively for complaints, systematic audits aim to identify areas of pay disparity by gender and race across the workforce so they can be rectified. Denmark stands out as a pioneer of legally requiring independent equal pay checks.

Many experts also highlight the value of pay scale standardization to establish clear compensation benchmarks for positions. Relying on subjective salary determinations enables unconscious bias. Posting uniform pay bands company-wide for different roles and seniority levels promotes fairness.

In recruiting, banning inquiries about applicants' salary history also shows promise for reducing discrimination. When past pay gets used to determine offers, it perpetuates biases entrenched in earlier career stages. Salary history thus must be blocked from consideration.

Numerous studies reveal that practices like anonymous hiring procedures curb gender biases. When demographic information gets masked during resume screening and interviews, women face better odds of advancement. Objective, structured interviews similarly prevent gender assumptions.

Equipping women to confidently negotiate pay and raises is essential. Since early compensation often anchors future earnings trajectories, empowering assertive bargaining helps secure higher initial offers rather than settling. Many organizations now provide negotiation skill training.

Among the most impactful company-level policies are extended, gender-neutral paid parental leaves and flexible work arrangements. When men also take substantial time off for caregiving, it helps women return to their careers rather than reducing hours or dropping out. Flexibility also aids retention.

Lastly, subsidized childcare availability relieves working parents of costly burdens weighing heavier on mothers. Affordable, quality options prevent women from leaving jobs due to family demands. On-site daycares take this a step further in convenience.

While no single solution creates instant parity, coordinated efforts across multiple areas provide hope. But lasting cultural change also relies on individuals reflecting on how we enable residual inequities. With combined will, equitably compensating women's contributions is possible.

CHAPTER 5: WOMEN IN LEADERSHIP

Despite comprising over half the population, women remain underrepresented in high-level leadership roles across sectors worldwide. The "glass ceiling" phenomenon upholds gendered imbalances in power and influence across government, business, academia, and more. Dismantling embedded structural biases requires coordinated efforts.

This chapter will examine statistics on women leaders, the barriers they uniquely face, and proven strategies for reaching equal representation. Realizing this vision hinges on empowering marginalized voices at all levels—from the boardroom to society as a whole.

<u>The State of Women Leaders</u>

While slow progress occurs, a stark leadership gap remains:

- Only 24 women serve as heads of government out of nearly 200 nations. Most nations have never elected a woman leader.

- Women make up less than 8% of national leaders worldwide, trailing most sectors.

- Just 37 of the world's 500 largest companies have a woman CEO. The share of women CEOs in America's top companies has stalled around 6-7% for two decades.

- Among Fortune 500 boards, women hold 28% of seats, up from 16% a decade prior. Countries like France, Norway and Spain have 40% minimums.

- In America, women comprise 30% of Congress and 30% of state legislatures. Only 8 states have female governors.

- At colleges, around 30% of presidents and 40% of faculty are women. Women only earn around 33% of engineering and computer science degrees.

While marginal gains occur, unwritten rules still govern leadership pipeline flows. Pockets of female leadership do exist, demonstrating possibility with intentional policy shifts.

Barriers Facing Women Leaders

While explicit discrimination has declined, a set of persistent barriers continue impeding women's leadership and advancement worldwide. Until these structural and social obstacles get dismantled, true gender balance across high-level positions will remain elusive.

Overt leadership discrimination has become less common and legally risky, yet evidence shows women still face biased recruiting and hiring processes, performance evaluations, promotion rates, and compensation practices. Subtle forms of favoritism toward male candidates, projects, and work styles reveal lingering prejudice among those controlling advancement pathways.

Female leaders also frequently find themselves excluded from influential informal social and professional development opportunities due to lingering "old boys club" cultural dynamics. Male-dominated networking activities and mentoring circles fail to provide the sponsorship, visibility, and insider expertise women need to climb the ladder. This isolation impedes growth.

The strain of balancing leadership with disproportionate family care burdens also disproportionately causes women to either slow down or pause advancement. Inflexible work norms coupled with societal expectations around parenting and domestic duties pull women off advancement trajectories. Supportive flexibility remains lacking.

Unconscious gender biases reinforce perceptions of leadership as inherently masculine. Traits viewed as strong in men may seem abrasive in women. Cultural concepts portray authority, dominance and strategy as masculine capabilities. Without realizing it, talent assessors apply gendered frames prescribing different leadership requirements for women versus men.

Relatedly, women leaders sometimes face tougher expectations and standards compared to male peers. Actions and leadership styles admired in male leaders may get criticized as overly domineering or aggressive in women. This sexual double standard creates added scrutiny.

Additionally, some senior women leaders embody "queen bee syndrome" where they feel pressured to distance themselves from more junior women and uphold male cultural norms. Rather than empower other women rising, they serve as gatekeepers for existing power structures.

Sexual harassment and dismissive, disrespectful treatment from colleagues and subordinates also uniquely burden women leaders. Gendered power issues taint critical mentoring and collegial relationships necessary for advancement. Simply navigating daily interpersonal dynamics requires added toll.

Finally, with so few women in upper ranks, those reaching senior levels feel isolated and tokenized in their field or company. Lacking a critical mass of female peers leads women feeling forced to downplay their identities or conform to masculine leadership conventions.

Myriad explanations exist for women's absence from leadership roles globally. But one thing is clear: removing the barriers and biases limiting their potential promises to strengthen economies, organizations, and society as a whole. The strategies to empower women leaders must match the scale of hurdles they face.

Effective Strategies to Empower Women Leaders

Individuals, organizations and governments globally must take initiative to cultivate women leadership, including:

Individual Level:

- Join women's professional networks for solidarity and mentorship.

- Seek both male and female mentors/sponsors.

- Negotiate equitable pay and flexible work options; use parental leave.

- Develop assertive communication and self-advocacy skills.

- When senior, purposefully mentor and advocate for other women

Organizational Level:

- Set diversity targets at all management levels, not just entry-level.

- Mitigate bias in recruiting and performance reviews.

- Offer unconscious bias and empathetic leadership training.

- Implement transparent pay scales; audit and address pay gaps.

- Establish paid parental leave policies, flexible work and onsite childcare.

- Sponsor rising women into high-profile assignments, boards and networks.

- Call out and penalize any harassment, talk of "boys clubs" etc.

Policy Level:

- Institute board gender quotas like those in Europe

- Pass equal pay and anti-discrimination legislation; enforce vigorously.

- Provide government subsidized childcare and extended parental leave.

- Support programs helping women gain qualifications and enter non-traditional fields.

- Finance and spotlight women entrepreneurs; mandate women-owned business targets

With collaborative action, we can disrupt past patterns and create a society where women and men equally share positions of authority and influence. The diverse perspectives this enables benefits organizations and communities. While work remains, a new generation of women leaders rises, reminding girls everywhere of their power.

CHAPTER 6: BALANCING FAMILY CAREGIVING ROLES

While social norms evolve, caregiving duties within families still disproportionately fall on women. Mothers continue accruing a "wage penalty" for domestic work while fathers gain a "bonus." However, studies show egalitarian approaches to balancing career and family benefit all.

This chapter explores the impacts of imbalanced domestic roles, the need for supportive work policies, and strategies for spreading caregiving responsibilities more equitably. Doing so enriches relationships while allowing both parents to thrive professionally.

The Motherhood Penalty vs. Fatherhood Bonus

Despite more women working, societal expectations of mothers and fathers stick to antiquated norms:

- Women's careers suffer after having children. One study found a 4% wage penalty per child among American women.

- Men experience an opposite "daddy bonus." Fathers earn over 6% more compared to childless male peers according to research.

- Employers demonstrate biases, viewing mothers as less competent and committed to their careers. Fathers face no such assumptions.

- While growing, only 23% of fathers take more than 2 weeks of paternity leave globally. Taking leave is stigmatized.

- Women spend 2-10 times more time on unpaid domestic work like childcare and housework, regardless of working status.

This imbalance results in less career progression and income growth for women overall, while men's earning trajectories benefit. True equality requires dismantling expectations of women as default caregivers.

The Need for Supportive Workplace Policies

Social norms interact with workplace structures, together disadvantaging mothers. Supportive policies make careers and caregiving compatible for both parents, including:

- Mandated paid parental leave – Nations with at least 6 months off for each parent, like Sweden and Norway, see the most equitable benefits.

- Flexible work options – Compressed schedules, remote work, and flexible hours allow caregiving without derailing careers.

- On-site childcare – Workplace daycare reduces logistical stresses of parenting young children.

- Anti-discrimination protection – Ensuring hiring, pay and promotion are free of motherhood bias.

- Career re-entry programs – Bridging any resume gaps after extended leave smooths workforce re-entry.

- Job sharing and part-time tracks –Allowing two parents to each work reduced hours accommodates families.

- Lactation rooms and breaks – Providing spaces and time for breastfeeding/pumping at work normalizes the practice.

Workplaces promoting egalitarian parenting do exist. But transforming outdated norms takes broadened policies along with shifting attitudes.

Strategies for Sharing Caregiving Equitably

Beyond policy and workplace changes, couples must take the initiative to equitably share domestic duties and childcare responsibilities as key to gender equality.

Here are some recommended strategies for purposefully spreading caregiving more evenly.

First, couples should proactively discuss values, priorities, and plans regarding career-family balance before having kids. Defining visions and intentions early provides a strong foundation. However, maintaining flexibility as realities emerge is crucial, since theories and best intentions often prove unrealistic post-birth. Open communication without rigid assumptions works best.

Fundamentally, partners must challenge ingrained gender role assumptions by de-gendering childcare and household tasks. Avoid defaulting into mom and dad responsibilities. Regardless of biological sex, both parents have equal capabilities for nurturance, bonding, play, discipline, chores, errands and more. Share all duties.

In a related vein, couples must vocally validate domestic labor as equally vital, not just the woman's domain. Society undervalues this unpaid work, signaling it as less important than paid office work. Yet smooth households underpin happy families and careers. Framing caregiving as every adult's responsibility combats outdated gender notions.

Setting a 50/50 split goal is unrealistic amid the complexities of daily life. However, generally taking initiative to balance duties until they subjectively feel fair, then periodically rechecking and adjusting, works well for many. The aim should be reasonable equity, not perfection.

Outsourcing help through childcare services, housecleaning, meal kits and more provides needed support during crunch times. View this as investing in the partnership, not failure or weakness. The point is not total self-reliance but sharing duties creatively.

When one partner is taking on more tasks, the other must proactively offer help and give them breaks. Saying "just tell me what you need" puts an added burden on the person carrying the load. Adopt a bias toward taking initiative and reducing their pressures.

Frequently check in together about how each person is coping with work-family demands and what they need to feel supported in the partnership. Listen without defensiveness. Make requests early before resentment builds.

Accepting interdependency strengthens families. Needing help is not failure or inadequacy—it is healthy and human. Letting go of ideals of parental self-sufficiency enables partners to lean on each other during times of need.

Lastly, individuals should prioritize occasional self-care. Burnout helps no one. Short-term solutions like childcare help, sleep, exercise, and breaks prevent the buildup of chronic stress over the long-term. Protect space for personal wellbeing.

With teamwork and intentionality, rebalancing gendered social norms around domestic roles is possible. The rewards for children witnessing a new model of shared parenting are immeasurable.

Reframing family care as a shared responsibility between men and women– biological or adopted - demonstrates mature manhood. Modeling this for the next generation can lead to their own equitable views of parenting. Policy reform combined with purposeful changes within families moves society forward.

Collapsing the Divide

Chapter 7: Gender-Based Violence

Around the world, women face shockingly high rates of violence due to their gender. These include sexual assault and domestic abuse at disproportionate levels. To combat gendered violence in all its forms, we must understand its root causes, uplift survivors' voices, and foster more accountable attitudes and norms.

This chapter will examine the global scope of violence against women, its societal underpinnings, the power of shared stories, and proven prevention strategies. The goal is not to instill fear, but galvanize action toward gender-based violence eradication.

Forms of Violence Against Women Globally

No nation is immune from violence targeting women for their gender. Forms include:

- Domestic abuse – Around 1 in 3 women experience physical or sexual violence from an intimate partner during their lifetime based on WHO estimates. Psychological abuse is even more widespread, used to control women and erode self-worth by abusive partners.

- Rape and sexual assault – These span acquaintance assaults on dates to violent attacks by strangers. Every 73 seconds another American is sexually assaulted according to RAINN. Globally, it is estimated only one third of attacks are reported—silencing many victims.

- Femicide – While more men in total are murdered, women face dramatically heightened risk of being killed by intimate partners. An estimated 50,000 women were killed in 2017 globally by partners or family members.

- Street harassment – Lewd comments, groping, and public intimidation of women is rampant. A recent U.S. study found 81% of women experience sexual harassment in some form in their lifetime.

- Human trafficking – Sex trafficking and forced prostitution exploit approximately 4.5 million people globally, disproportionately women and girls.

- workplace harassment – Beyond typical harassment, sexual coercion and assault remains common. EEOC data finds women file 75-85% of sexual harassment claims in America.

- Honor killings – Women murdered by family members "in defense of cultural purity" still occur in places like the Middle East and South Asia.

- Dowry killings – Brides murdered over disputes related to dowry demands still plague sections of India. Estimates suggest at least one death per hour.

- Female infanticide – Preferences for sons over daughters leads to as many 100 million missing female births in Asia and Africa over 30 years according to UN estimates.

This small sampling makes the pervasive scope of gendered violence clear. Its roots run deep through social forces we must confront.

Cultural and Structural Foundations

All forms of violence against women stem from the same core driver: Societal norms endorsing male aggression and control over women's autonomy. Specific cultural ingredients enabling violence include:

- Sexist gender roles – Rigid norms create dominant men and subordinate women. Violence polices gender boundaries.

- Culture of female purity – Concepts of stained "honor" justify violence to restore men's status. Victims get blamed.

- Women as property – Treating women as objects to be claimed enables abuse, trafficking, and restricted rights.

- Culture of male strength – Violence perceived as natural for men gets excused as inherent biology, rather than socialized behavior.

- Culture of silence – Stigma prevents women speaking out about abuse and officials taking action.

- Victim blaming – Focus put on women's behavior ("Why was she there?") rather than perpetrators' choices.

- Lack of legal protections – Inadequate laws on gender violence, marital rape, trafficking, and female property rights perpetuate vulnerabilities.

Sexist cultural attitudes drive violence. But regressive social structures and policies enable its persistence. Transforming these empowers women and creates accountability.

Amplifying Survivors' Voices

"Me Too" spotlights the power of survivors bravely sharing their stories to wake society up. Some courageous voices speaking out include:

- Author Chanel Miller revealed her identity after brock turner's 2016 assault. Her book Know My Name sparked advocacy.

- Tarana Burke founded the Me-Too movement in 2007 to support survivors, predominantly women of color. It gained global traction in 2017.

- Writer and activist Gloria Steinem drew attention to domestic violence with pioneering 1970s articles and women's shelters.

- Nobel laureate Malala Yousafzai survived a Taliban assassination attempt for demanding girls' education. Her activism continues.

- Software engineer Susan Fowler detailed workplace sexism at Uber in a viral 2017 blog post, helping spur change.

- Actress Angelina Jolie shares her domestic violence experiences and advocates for abused women through film and law.

- Musician Lady Gaga, herself a survivor, recorded empowering ballad Til It Happens to You for campus assault documentary The Hunting Ground.

Each story chips away at stigma and isolation. Combined, they reveal systemic injustice both calling for and enabling change. We all gain courage and wisdom from survivor testimonies.

Strategies for Prevention and Accountability

Ending gendered violence requires action across all areas it is condoned:

- Change attitudes and norms – Teach gender equality from early ages. Engage men against toxic masculinity. Debunk victim-blaming mindsets.

- Update inadequate laws – Pass comprehensive policies on domestic violence, marital rape, trafficking, harassment, property rights and protections. Enforce them.

- Train law enforcement – Many dissatisfied survivors find police dismissive and unresponsive. Officers require education on trauma-informed, victim-centered handling.

- Provide support services – Women's shelters, hotlines, legal aid, counseling and outreach programs are severely underfunded in most regions. Support access.

- Ensure workplace safety – Implement clear sexual harassment policies; conduct bias training. Take reports extremely seriously with proportionate consequences.

- Increase female empowerment – Ensure girls' education access worldwide. Support programs teaching women self-defense, legal knowledge, job skills and financial independence.

- Spotlight positive models – Male allies and youth leaders should vocally model respect and equality. Highlight healthy masculinities.

With coordinated action across multiple fronts, we can envision a world where gender no longer determines safety - where girls become women without threat of violence. The goal seems far, yet it also feels within reach as more find the conviction to act.

Collapsing the Divide

Chapter 8: Intersectionality and Inclusion

While this book examines gender inequality and identity, these issues intersect with other forms of marginalization including race, class, sexual orientation, ability and age. The interplay between these systems of oppression shapes lived experiences in multidimensional ways based on one's social position.

This concluding chapter explores the impacts of intersecting biases, highlights diverse voices, and reaffirms the need for radical inclusion in our laws, policies and social fabric. Only by embracing people across all gender identities and social groups can we achieve a just society.

<u>Interconnected Forces of Oppression</u>

Gender discrimination intersects with the following forces in society:

- Racism – Women of color face double discrimination, evident in disproportionate violence, pay gaps, health disparities, over-policing and more.

- Classism – Economic inequality amplifies gender inequality. Lower income women lack resources to escape abusive situations, attain education, or advance careers.

- Homophobia – Alongside transphobia, same-sex attracted and non-binary individuals endure added vulnerabilities to bullying, homelessness, workplace exclusion or health risks.

- Ableism – Women with disabilities or serious illnesses are more likely to experience abuse and exclusions from jobs/social access. Stigma persists.

- Ageism – Young women may lack power and status while older women become culturally "invisible," facing employment barriers and social marginalization.

- Xenophobia – Immigrant women and refugees endure stereotyping, discrimination in the workplace, barriers to resources, and risk of detention/deportation.

Gender cannot be examined in isolation from the above forces which shape societal status and wellbeing. Solutions addressing gender inequality must be inclusive of intersecting injustices. No one is free until all are free.

Unique Pain Points of Diverse Groups

Here are just some examples of multidimensional impacts felt at the intersection of gender and other attributes:

When examining the impacts of gender inequality, it quickly becomes clear they are not felt evenly across demographics. The interplay between gender and other attributes like race, sexual orientation, class, ability, and age creates unique pain points and vulnerabilities facing specific populations.

For women marginalized by race or ethnicity, gender discrimination compounds with entrenched biases tied to identity. Black, Latina, Native American and other women of color consistently earn lower wages for the same work compared to white men and women. Racist stereotypes fuel harmful assumptions around competence and worth. Minority women also face disproportionate rates of workplace harassment and violence, while lacking equitable access to healthcare, education, political representation and justice.

Within the LGBTQ community, gender manifests complexly. While gay men experience privilege along gender lines, they confront assumptions of effeminacy and gender nonconformity. Lesbians battle simultaneous sexism and homophobia that doubly disadvantage careers, relationships, and social acceptance. Bisexual individuals face erasure and questioning of the validity of their identity. Most severely marginalized are transgender and non-binary folks who navigate systemic transphobia and exclusion daily.

Socioeconomic class strongly intersects with gender given the widespread poverty among single mothers struggling with childcare, unpredictable low-wage work, inadequate healthcare, housing insecurity, unreliable transportation, and other survival challenges while attempting to better their families. Greater workplace protections and social supports provide lifelines to keep women out of poverty.

For women with disabilities or serious illnesses, additional barriers exist to healthcare, accessible public transit, shelters, reproductive rights, and employment. Ableist assumptions questioning capabilities magnify gendered disadvantages. Women fighting disabilities or diseases must battle baseline sexism on top of stigma surrounding their health or abilities that constrain socioeconomic options.

Young women contend with paternalism and dismissal of their perspectives due to lack of experience, while also facing high rates of school harassment and self-esteem issues in adolescence. At the other end of the spectrum, older women confront ageist biases around tech skills, energy, memory, and competence that obstruct hiring and advancement. Elder women further deal with invisibility and isolation as they get categorized outside definitions of beauty and vitality.

Immigrant and undocumented women wrestle with the vulnerabilities of unstable legal status and exploitative employers in addition to sexism. Xenophobic profiling also marginalizes certain ethnic groups more than others, especially women wearing religious garb. Language barriers, lack of childcare support, and cultural assimilation challenges compound gender inequality.

These represent just a few examples illustrating that due to intersectionality, inequality manifests in multidimensional ways. Well-intentioned efforts toward women's empowerment often focus narrowly on white, middle-class, native-born, able-bodied, heterosexual experiences. But progress means ensuring marginalized women do not continue falling through the cracks—seen but not heard. An inclusive feminist future beckons us to embrace nuanced solutions addressing the needs of diverse populations.

Understanding these unique challenges sparks more compassionate, tailored policy and cultural change.

<u>Recognizing Diverse Experiences</u>

Here are just some of the many brave voices sharing their distinct stories and advocating for intersectional gender justice:

- Activist Tarana Burke centers the experiences of working-class women of color in the MeToo movement.

- Writer Roxane Gay provides insights into navigating the world as a black bisexual woman in Bad Feminist and other works.

- Actress Geena Davis advocates reducing ageist stereotypes in media and provides opportunities for older actresses through her Institute on Gender in Media.

- Advocate Munroe Bergdorf calls attention to the layers of discrimination facing black transgender women.
- Activist Dolores Huerta organizes Latina immigrant farmworkers around workers' rights and reproductive justice.

- Politician Alexandria Ocasio-Cortez stresses the economic dimensions of gender equality.

- Writer Corinne Lee chronicles the erasure of disabled women's experiences and activism.

- Organizer Sylvia Rivera fought for acceptance of low-income, racial minority trans individuals at the 1969 Stonewall Riots.

Each perspective expands our understanding of gender's multidimensional impacts. Inclusion requires elevating voices from all backgrounds to shape solutions meeting their needs and realities.

The Road Ahead for True Inclusion

While meaningful progress occurs daily, transformational change embracing diverse gender identities and experiences remains needed across institutions and systems including:

Laws and Policies - Comprehensive anti-discrimination legislation must protect people from identity-based mistreatment and lack of accommodation in employment, healthcare, housing, banking, government services, education, and all public accommodations. Holistic laws send a clear statement of cultural values. We must also expand social support services and resources for populations facing compound vulnerabilities. Policy establishes the scaffolding for equality.

Businesses - The public and nonprofit sectors shoulder significant responsibility for equitable, inclusive environments. Human resource practices must be analyzed to ensure fair and bias-free recruiting, hiring, assignments, evaluations, compensation, promotions, and benefits regardless of gender, race, age, health and other aspects across all staff levels. Anti-harassment training fosters respectful culture, along with showcasing diverse leadership.

Media Representation - The narratives, images and voices amplified through news, film, television, literature and advertising shape perceptions and possibilities. While slow improvements occur, we must push for more authentic, humanized depictions that counteract singular stereotypes and celebrate the spectrum of intersectional experiences. This expands imagination.

Education - Schools bear unique responsibility to raise enlightened generations, teaching intersectional sensitivity and identities from early ages. All children deserve learning environments where they feel secured, valued and free to explore individual interests and strengths without judgment, limited expectations or social bullying. This is the foundation of progress.

Healthcare - Quality, affordable healthcare enables people to thrive in all other areas of life. We must tailor services to physical and mental health needs of diverse populations, while confronting historic exclusion and discrimination in medical institutions. Cultural competence, reproductive care access and support for gender transitions remain essential.

Community Support Systems - Grassroots groups providing critical services and a sense of community for marginalized folks fill gaps left by mainstream institutions. We must support and donate to identity-specific resource centers, shelters, hotlines, counseling services, legal aid groups, workforce programs, youth support groups, and outreach networks that uplift lives.

In essence, every facet of society must reexamine systems and norms that intentionally include some groups yet oppress others. This spans from interpersonal interactions to giant bureaucratic structures. While government legislation sets standards, individuals too must reflect on our biases, assumptions and patterns enabling inequity. We inherit centuries of injustice; transforming society requires commitment across all levels.

At times this work feels overwhelming, given the scale of entrenched disparities and resistance to change. But we must remember that empowering the most marginalized people benefits everyone, bringing us closer to the full human potential and creativity a liberated world promises. Though the path stretches far ahead, we walk it together step by step.

A just future beckons us toward greater complexity of thinking, connection across differences, and radical inclusion of people of all genders and identities. Though the path stretches far ahead, we walk it with shared hope that each step takes us closer.